LISTEN!

LEARN ABOUT SOUND

BY PAMELA HALL

The Child's World

Published by The Child's World®
1980 Lookout Drive • Mankato, MN 56003-1705
800-599-READ • www.childsworld.com

ACKNOWLEDGMENTS
The Child's World®: Mary Berendes, Publishing Director
Content Consultant: Paul Ohmann, PhD, Associate Professor of Physics,
    University of St. Thomas
The Design Lab: Design and production
Red Line Editorial: Editorial direction

PHOTO CREDITS: Nicole S. Young/iStockphoto, cover, 1, 2, 3, 4, 6, 8, 10, 12,
14, 16, 18, 20, 22; Galina Barskaya/Fotolia, 5, 21 (top); Fotolia, 7, 9; Lesley
Lister/iStockphoto, 11 (top); Luis Carlos Torres/iStockphoto, 11 (bottom); Dmitry
Mordvintsev/iStockphoto, 13 (top); David H. Lewis/iStockphoto, 13 (bottom);
Mark Bond/Fotolia, 15; Jani Bryson/iStockphoto, 17; Peter Eckhardt/iStockphoto,
19; Peter Schinck/Fotolia, 21 (bottom); Jane Yamada, 23

LIBRARY OF CONGRESS CATALOGING-IN-PUBLICATION DATA
Hall, Pamela.
  Listen! Learn about sound / by Pamela Hall ; illustrated by Jane Yamada.
    p. cm.
  ISBN 978-1-60253-510-7 (lib. bd. : alk. paper)
  1. Sound—Juvenile literature. 2. Sound-waves—Juvenile literature. I. Yamada,
Jane, ill. II. Title.
  QC225.5.H35 2010
  534—dc22   2010010978

Printed in the United States of America in Mankato, Minnesota.
July 2010
F11538

CONTENTS

Create Vibrations

What sounds have you made today?
Did you hum or sing?
Did you whisper or shout?
Did you stomp your feet
or bang a drum?

All of those sounds began the same
way—with a **vibration**. A vibration is
a special way that something moves.

Blowing air into a flute creates vibrations. ▶

Bang a hammer and it vibrates.
It moves back and forth very fast,
but ever so slightly.

The hammer shakes the air around it.
Vibrations move through the air
in **invisible** waves.

You can't see
the hammer
vibrating. But
you may feel
the movement
in your hand. ▶

Imagine a rock tossed into a still pond. See the rings of waves in the water? Sound waves move away from the hammer the way the water ripples away from the rock.

Sound waves go on and on until they run out of energy.

Sound waves move like these ripples. However, sound travels in all directions, not just across one flat surface. ▶

Listen Up

Are you close enough to the sound waves? If you are, tiny bones in your ear will vibrate.

The vibrations are turned into signals that go to your brain. Your brain figures out what the sound is.

Some sounds make us happy, such as laughter or music. ▶

Some noises annoy us, such as a buzzing fly. ▶

What makes some sounds high?
Things that make high sounds
vibrate very fast. The sound waves
are close together.

Things that vibrate slowly
make lower sounds.
The sound waves are farther apart.

A violin makes
high notes. ▶

A sousaphone
makes low
notes. ▶

12

Why are some sounds loud?
The waves are big!

Softer sounds have smaller waves.

Ouch! Protect
your ears
when sounds
are loud. ▶

14

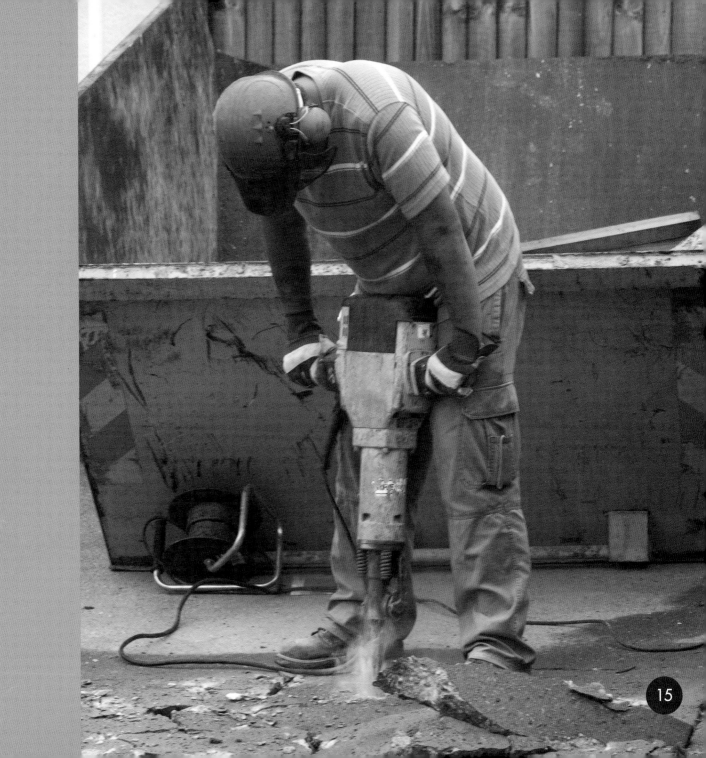

15

Make Some Noise

Put your hand on your throat and hum.
Can you feel your **vocal cords** vibrate?
The air around them vibrates, too.
Your voice is carried away on waves
of sound.

Now you're talking!

Vocal cords are folds of tissue inside your throat. They vibrate when you sing. ▶

16

Hello, Hello, Hello, Hello, Hello.

Have you ever heard your **echo**?
Maybe you were in a big,
empty room or a giant cave.
The sound of your voice bounced off
the walls and came back to you.

Sound All Around

Our voices aren't the only way we use sound to **communicate**. Cell phones ring. We clap and cheer if we are excited. Sirens warn us to watch out.

Animals use sound, too. They chatter, chirp, hiss, and growl.

Babies communicate by crying. ▶

Dolphins make whistling and clicking sounds that travel far underwater. ▶

Low, high, loud, soft—sound
is all around you.

How are these sounds different?
    A siren,
    thunder,
    a squeaky door,
    and a purring cat?

Keep listening for sounds. *Swish*.
Can you hear your page turning now?

Low, High, Loud, Soft

Low sounds have waves that are far apart.

pom-pom-po-dum

High sounds have waves that are closer together.

tweeeeet

Loud sounds have big waves.

roar

Soft sounds have smaller waves.

swish

Words to Know

communicate (ka-MYOO-nih-kayt): To communicate is to share information through talking, writing, or other ways. We use sound to communicate.

echo (EH-koh): An echo is a sound that bounces back to you. To hear your echo, you need lots of empty space and a big surface, such as a building or a mountain.

invisible (in-VIZ-ah-bul): Something invisible cannot be seen. Sound waves are invisible.

vibration (veye-BRAY-shun): A vibration is when something moves back and forth ever so slightly but also very quickly. Vibrations create sound waves.

vocal cords (VOH-kal KORDZ): Vocal cords are folds of tissue inside your throat. Vocal cords vibrate to help you speak.